"If you are lookin[g]
and don't know w[...]

NO MONEY DOWN

Your Path to Real Estate Investing with No or Low Down Payment

Scott Whitwam

No Money Down

Your Path to Real Estate Investing With No or Low Down Payment

by

Scott Whitwam

29 28 27 26 25 24   1 2 3 4 5 6

NO MONEY DOWN: Your Path to Real Estate Investing
With No or Low Down Payment

Author Disclaimer:
Every effort has been made to accurately represent the skills, concepts, ideas, techniques, and "know-how" offered by Scott Whitwam and his potential. There is no guarantee that you will earn any money using the techniques and ideas in these materials. Examples in these materials are not to be interpreted as a promise or guarantee of earnings. Earning potential is entirely dependent on the person using our product, ideas and techniques. We do not purport this as a "get rich scheme."

Your level of success in attaining the results claimed in our materials depends on the time you devote to the program, ideas and techniques mentioned, your finances, knowledge and various skills. Since these factors differ according to individuals, we cannot guarantee your success or income level, nor are we responsible for any of your actions.

As always, we recommend you consult qualified financial and legal professionals before pursuing any actions to determine suitability for your specific situation.

Published by:
Emerge Publishing, LLC
9521B Riverside Parkway, Suite 243
Tulsa, Oklahoma 74137
www.Emerge.pub

ISBN: 978-1-954-96638-3

BISAC Category:
BUS054010   BUSINESS & ECONOMICS / Real Estate / Buying & Selling Homes
BUS036050   BUSINESS & ECONOMICS / Investments & Securities / Real Estate

Printed in the United States

TABLE OF CONTENTS

CHAPTER 1

Why Should You Listen to Me?

A lazy person complains about not having money and tries to get rich quickly. A diligent person builds wealth through proper planning and attention to their goals. (Prov 10:4 & 21:5)

Having knowledge is helpful, with it you can work and build an average life. Knowing how to apply the knowledge you have accumulated is called wisdom or understanding, and with wisdom and understanding, you can achieve nearly anything you can dream. Wisdom and understanding are a shield when you face your most difficult times in life.

It is one thing to know what to do and another thing to know why to do it, this [wisdom-understanding] can turn around any situation. Unfortunately, I have never found it to be instant, cheap or easy to gain the wisdom and understanding that you need.

As a Real Estate Coach, Investor, and Broker I know how hard and discouraging it is when trying to find trusted help and transformational information… even from the "experts" that you are paying to help you!

In this, I am no different than you. I have read volumes of books, attended seminar after seminar, networked, and spent a fortune on lots of mass-sold systems and programs that failed to move me any closer to the results I desired.

I started my first business at age 14 with no training, obviously no experience, no money, and a high school teacher as my only mentor. I had no idea how to run a business.

Since then, I have started over 15 successful businesses in multiple highly competitive industries. However, when I got started I had more dreams than money, you could say I had deep pockets and very short arms.

The process of educating myself to become successful at real estate investing was painful!

After I graduated from trade school, I got a job but I knew I was meant for so much more. Then I started a side business, but my wife and I could barely pay the bills! I was not making the kind of money I was expecting. I thought that I could do better if I went full-time in my own business.

It took months of exhausting 18-hour days, but it seemed that all the profits went to leases, new equipment, and inventory… the results were slow and small.

I thought, "I must be doing something wrong. I need a mentor. Someone experienced who can help me."

I knew I needed help and I began to seek experts who had proven expertise and could tell me what I needed to do. But who was I as a young inexperienced guy with a big dream and no money? The people I needed to learn from had already achieved a level of success and were hanging out with others like themselves. I couldn't get face time with the experts as they were way too busy for me and I didn't fit into their social group.

I get it, they had better things to do than spend time helping me and investing in my dreams. I was someone who could become their competitor!

So now what?

I decided to take action. I began to seek out the "experts" who were willing to address my questions, teach me, and speak to the concerns I was dealing with. I found them very eager to help and share their secrets... IF I would just buy their books and audio recordings, go to their seminars, and purchase their products and training programs.

So, I did it. I spent lots of money on programs that had great promises from people who knew how to sell their stuff. However, it failed to move me closer to where I wanted to be and left me even more frustrated than before. Where was the real meaningful help? Where was the guide that showed them how to do it step by step?

There seemed to be no shortage of self-proclaimed know-it-alls, each selling programs that talked about the breaks they got, the money they made, the cars they drove, and the houses they owned. And they were charging premium prices of $3,000, $10,000, $20,000, and more. Ultimately, there was not much help to get me to the place where they were.

You shouldn't have to go through that, because I already paid the price, felt the frustration, and wasted a ton of time...

I'm not saying all the "experts" in real estate are bad – there are many good coaches out there. But for the most part, they are selling overpriced trash, that is incomplete, complex, and confusing.

It has always been incomprehensible to me how someone can produce a dozen audio or video trainings with workbooks, tips, and simple forms and a how-to guide, sell it for $5,000 or more and leave you more confused than before, and wondering how you go ripped off this time.

The one day it came to me, it hit me like a line drive...

These experts have the motivation to do it! It is on PURPOSE.

If the experts can keep us from knowing the stepping stones needed to succeed we will continue to buy their "secret sauce." Once we finally figure it out, we don't have to keep shelling out cash for their products. That's why they fail to include key pieces to the puzzle.

Then you continue to go from one hope to another hope without obtaining the success you were promised.

Let me let you in on a secret – they will never give you all the pieces needed... Every surefire answer leads to another unanswered obstacle that requires you to buy another seminar or program. And guess what – they charge you a premium to get another needed step in the process.

They promise fame, fortune, and happiness, but they never actually tell you how to get it.

These trainers intentionally make assurances that they know cannot be kept. This I can promise you without hesitation.

I will never treat people that way.

If you want to know something, I will be upfront and answer what I know about the subject – direct answers only! And if I don't know an answer, then I will put you in contact with someone who does.

The experts had taken my money, given me very little, and disappointed me. Over time, I was out of money and options… they were rich and I was still needing direction.

This forced me to figure it out on my own. The process was grueling, painful, expensive, and cost me years to figure out by trial and error.

There is no doubt that it was all worth it.

The reason I want to share with you this information is not to make you feel sorry for me or tout how successful I have become. I wanted you to know and understand how discouraging and frustrating it can be to break the code in an industry that thrives on keeping you from succeeding.

I also know how to be successful in this industry. It is not just theory, but something I have done–not just for a couple of years, but for decades.

I would like to share a personal story with you.

As a young aspiring businessperson, I was invited to a "guru" meeting billed to be much like other meetings I had attended. I heard information about how I could break out of mediocrity and become successful and develop a proven financial strategy for success. I'm sure it is like the expert seminars you have been to before.

For me, money was tight but when given the opportunity I purchased the whole program being pitched. As the last session closed a friend said he was going to the elite member's bonus session and dinner.

I said "wait... I want in".

I knew nothing about a bonus session, and it wasn't mentioned on the platform, or if it was, I missed it. I turned around and the conference host was at his product table, so I walked over and asked if I could attend the elite member's bonus session. After all, I had just purchased his success kit with all the information that was going to skyrocket me to financial freedom.

He said there were a couple of seats left for the elite students. I asked him how much it cost to join his elite program.

"OUCH!" - When he told me the price, I knew I couldn't afford it right then. But, I also knew that over the next couple of months, I would be able to afford it.

I asked if I could go now and pay later, after all, I had just thrown a wad of cash down at his table, and his response changed my life forever.

No.

He went on to tell me, that this was an exclusive elite group, and it would not be right to let me attend when everyone else had to pay a price to be there.

I was devastated for about 5 minutes and then after my 5-minute pity party concluded, I made the conscious decision this would never happen to me again. Within 2 months, I was able to join the elite program.

I was willing to pay the price to get where I needed to be.

Now it is me who truly wishes I could help other people do it for free. Here is a powerful lesson that I have learned.

If you're not willing to pay the price, you will not be willing to do the work required when problems, hard times or your "impossible" arises.

Thirty-five years later, he is still my number one coach, now a trusted mentor and also a personal friend.

For years, I have been asked to coach people, speak at events and share how I have done it. I am not a seeker of fame, I have chosen to focus on my family and other priorities that have brought me personal satisfaction and joy.

Fast forward to years later and after speaking on countless stages and building several profitable businesses in my lifetime, one day I was thinking and praying about how I could give out of my abundance and impact the lives of others.

I was struck with an epiphany...

There are a lot of wonderful people out there with the same dreams I once had, who are just like me when I began this journey. They have the same desires just as I did, with no one there to help them, to guide them and to share with them the tools and strategies that I was blessed to discover.

Who is going to help them in the way I was helped?

Suddenly, I felt a shift in my thinking. Maybe I am called to impart these keys and strategies that I have learned. But, how would I do that? The answer came to me immediately and the message was crystal clear: I can impact the lives of others through the process of one-on-one coaching and empower others with the tools and strategies needed to be a successful real estate investor. Nothing missing - not like the Gurus I had encountered early in my journey!

I really believe I have been called to help you!

I have used the last few years to focus on helping people learn the complicated business of real estate investing.

Now I have helped others just like you, to fulfill their real estate investing dreams and make game-changing money.

But this book isn't about me… it's about YOU!

We all need a road map to reach our destination and that is what the rest of the book is about - a road map to your future and an exciting future for you and your family. I'm going to show you how to take the steps one at a time and how to make game-changing money. It's time to let me show you how to develop wealth and create an exciting life.

The next few chapters will show you the ABCs of no-money-down real estate investing and how to turn your dream into reality. If you choose to read and absorb these strategies, this knowledge will take you from "hourly income" to "Game Changing Money."

You'll get the top secrets that successful real estate investors use that will enable you to maximize your strategies and much more!

Are You Ready?

You are about to uncover the way to have the life you love by doing something that is incredibly enjoyable.

CHAPTER 2

Introduction to No Money Down

The no-money-down real estate investing concept is not a new one. It may be new to you as it was to me when I stumbled onto it.

Like so many other investing strategies there is not just one "no money-down" model. The idea is more of a concept "a plan or idea" than a means of action. For instance, a seller may be the initiating party to a no-money-down transaction to maximize some tax strategy. A buyer may be offered the opportunity to purchase a property in this situation with zero money down.

This is a good place to make sure we cover a few misconceptions related to the "no money down model."

No money down real estate investing does not mean it is without cost. We are talking about a strategy that reduces or eliminates the need for a large down payment to purchase investment properties.

Traditional investor financing requires 20% to 50% down. In addition to the downpayment, you will have costs related to closing "closing costs". Many first-time investors are blindsided with potential expenses related to acquiring the title. Even though I have developed strategies for mitigating these and teach these techniques in our coaching program and courses, this book will not. Like my dad used to say...

"There is no such thing as a free lunch"

As an investor, it would be advisable to fully evaluate the opportunity in light of your investing goals. Not every no-money-down opportunity is a good one, depending on many factors beyond the down payment requirement like acquisition cost, deferred costs, cost of debt or interest rate, maturity or balloon, pre-payment fees, and deed or use restrictions are some of the factors an investor must consider.

There are some available no-money-down financing options that I don't spend a lot of time addressing in this book. These would be traditional no-money-down financing options where most competent mortgage lenders could explain how the programs work in great detail, as the specifics change with public policy.

A few of these loan types would be a VA loan for current and former military personnel, a USDA Home Loan, and some newer first-time home buyer programs. These are designed to be more retail products to aid homeowners but can also be used in certain circumstances for investing. An example may be a VA loan for a duplex in which the purchaser intends to live in one of the units and rent the other unit.

And even though I have coached people investing in using some of these retail loan programs, I consider them to be less creative than some of the other no money down real estate investing strategies.

However, most of the best deals and greatest opportunities do not qualify for retail lending products when they are required. These are the deals that I like best. Not because they can be more complicated, require more creativity, and generally look like lost causes, the reason I like these is because I don't generally have to provide a financial x-ray of my life and businesses.

I get asked with regularity what kind of properties can buyers with little or no money down purchase?

The answer is pretty simple:

"You can buy any property with zero money down that you can negotiate into a no-money-down deal."

CHAPTER 3

Understanding Creative Financing

I LOVE THE TERM CREATIVE FINANCING. In part because I have very little artistic creativity. On the other hand, my wife has enough artistic creativity for both of us. So the fact that I can be creative at all, even if it is in the wealth area, I'll take it.

I started to learn about creative financing back in my early business days in the 1980s. From understanding revolving credit, early pay discounts, flooring, and inventory leverage. It was this creativity at a time when there were no cell phones, no internet, and very few ways to learn real estate investing creativity that I put my first creative financing deal together.

Creative financing is the art of structuring a transaction in such a way that it bypasses or no longer needs traditional forms of financing. In one of my early retail businesses, auto parts, we were challenged to keep high-performance products in quantity and scope to give us an advantage over competing specialty shops and chain stores. In the process of looking for advantages, how we could better leverage our cash and credit to give us an advantage. I came across a wholesale supplier that was willing to provide some creative financing options. Traditionally a family-owned auto part store would either use company cash, go to a bank for an inventory loan, or establish a revolving 30-day credit account with the supply houses. The creative financing option that we settled on allowed us up to 90 days to pay, a discount if paid early, and the ability to pay by credit card tied to a rewards point program for free travel. This one creative financing option gave us an advantage in the marketplace and increased our income.

Okay, enough about auto parts. Using this same theory of creativity got me started as a real estate investor. In my case, I purchased at a discount a property that I always wanted to own, with terms that benefited me. I will share more about this particular type of acquisition in ***Chapter 5: Creative Financing Case Studies*** but let me share the nuts and bolts of the process here.

First, I found a property that matched the principle I stated earlier:

"You can buy any property with zero money down that you can negotiate into a no-money-down deal."

I not only identified a property that fit my buying criteria, location, size, and use, but it was one that likely would not qualify for traditional financing. Though I didn't know it at the time, there had been a fire in one of the bedrooms that the seller was unwilling to repair. Banks don't like homes that are not move-in ready. Something else I discovered but didn't know at the time was the property had just completed a private part foreclosure. This property was ripe for creative financing. Now the challenge that I had was to convince a seller that it was in their best interest to sell me the home with no money down.

How would I do that? I hadn't taken a course on real estate investing, never been taught how to buy real estate with zero down. I had heard about it though, so I knew it was possible. This friend once said, there are three things that are involved in every deal but you only need two of them and some creativity to put a deal together. Money, Credibility (reputation), and Credit. If you have a great reputation and great credit you generally can get the money. Money and credit can often provide you the credibility. And if you have money and credibility often you can acquire the credit.

But what do you do when you have none of those?

In my case, that was where I was at. My credit was shot from the expansion of our manufacturing activities, the person who was selling the property didn't know me and lived and ran a business over an hour from my stomping grounds. The third problem was that we were strapped for cash with the company expansion.

There is a passage in the Bible that says:

"You have not because you ask not."

Armed with everything I knew, I made my pitch. I likely sounded like a young, inexperienced dreamer... certainly not like a sophisticated, confident investor. Maybe that worked in my favor as I made my proposal.

This is my memory of the events and not an exact transcript:

> ***ME****: Sir, I would like to buy the property you have for sale. How much are you asking?*
>
> ***SELLER****: I want $120,000 cash.*
>
> ***ME****: Interesting, we definitely want to buy it, but I have one problem, I don't have any money. Would you carry a note with nothing down?*
>
> *We have a business that cash flows and I'm positive we will be able to pay it off in 3 to 5 years. [I had no idea if I would be able to do this, and he just*

foreclosed on some other sap who couldn't pay him what was owed.]

***SELLER**: [I remember the pause] I have a problem. I just foreclosed on the property and I gave the other person several months to empty the place out. I'm not making any repairs or doing any cleanup of the property. [Notice that there was not one question about my credit or my reputation and he knew I had no cash!]*

***ME**: That works for me. I'll give you the $120,000 with nothing down as a lease option, $7XX a month, and a 3-year balloon payoff.*

***SELLER**: You write the deal up and bring it to me to sign.*

This is one of my favorite stories because it is not something I heard, it is something I did. It happened, and it changed my entire approach to real estate investing. Over the years I have found many ways to buy no money down, in fact, this is my least used way but it still works.

Unlike my first deal, I don't use the approach of telling a seller that I have no money anymore. It really wasn't the best approach back then but I have always believed that honesty is the best policy. That does not mean you need to share all the dirty laundry with potential sellers. For instance, a couple of years back we were leveraging multiple transactions and I didn't feel compelled to tell the sellers that on paper we did not have the liquid cash in the accounts to satisfy the capital contributors required. It would have just scared them all away. We used our ability to creatively leverage the properties and ultimately completed multiple deals with zero money down.

There are many other creative ways to buy for no money down and here are some examples:

- Lease option
- Rent to own
- Seller carry back
- Wrap or subject to
- Hard money seller hold back
- Seller carry
- Joint venture

Each one of these methods requires different paperwork and structure. Enough so, that whole chapters or even books could be written about each no money down method. I share these so you're not tempted to think there is only one way to make this type of deal work. Unless you don't have the available cash to put down on a real estate purchase, I would not limit yourself to only no money down purchases. Though they are my preferred way of acquiring real estate sometimes the numbers are just too good putting money down or purchasing with cash. Both of which increase risk and reduce liquidity. Hence the avoidance when possible.

CHAPTER 4

Identifying No Money Down

When it comes to identifying no-money-down opportunities, I would say this is a blend of art and science. For forty years I have been told by sellers, investors, family, and friends what can't be done. Everybody seems to be an expert in not doing something or finding the problems that keep them from doing something. If you want to be a successful real estate investor who buys properties with zero down then you need to start finding the opportunities and possibilities in every transaction.

Here are three sources for identifying no-money-down deals:

Multiple Listing Service (MLS®)

There are many places you can find no money down opportunities including the local areas Multiple Listing Service "MLS®" if you look hard enough. If you do choose to buy properties using this platform you may end up paying a real estate agent commission for their assisting with the transaction. I have no issue with this as I own an investor-friendly real estate brokerage and know how hard my team works to help investors. With that said, most real estate agents do not understand creative financing and certainly do not understand no money down real estate investing and this can become an obstacle instead of an aid in putting together a transaction.

Even so, I do recommend that every investor have an investor-savvy real estate agent with MLS access that they can call on for assistance. Most associations have the ability for their Realtors® to provide investors search access in the system. Agents can also provide valuable research services and therefore should be paid for their efforts. You need to maintain control of all your transactions and not let a gung-ho agent derail your deals.

So what kind of no money down opportunities are advertising in the MLS? Generally none. They are hidden beneath the standard real estate agent listing information. Remember sellers hire real estate agents for their experience and ability to get retail pricing for properties. I have never had a seller call my brokerage office and ask for an agent who can sell their property for less money on buyer-friendly terms. No, generally they want more than retail, all cash, and no concessions. As an investor, we need to expect that most properties sell for retail price and terms to a retail buyer. This could be an owner-occupant or an investor. As an investor, you are looking for a motivated and flexible seller. So terms like "owner financing", "lease option", "rent to own", "seller carry back" and similar terms can show either motivation or flexibility in a seller. It can also be an investor who has learned the art of maximizing profits using these same creative options on the seller's side.

As an investor, you will need to get used to hearing "no" and that is ok. With every no, you are one offer closer to a yes.

"You miss 100% of the shots you do not take."

Attributed to Wayne Gretzky

So how do you screen some of the more likely candidates for properties and sellers on the MLS? You look at properties that nobody else is looking at.

The properties that have a higher number of days on the market, expired listings and canceled listings will generally meet this criteria. Time is a great motivator when it comes to sellers. The longer they hold a property they are trying to sell, the more it costs. You could become a creative rescuer.

The reason I wanted to start with the MLS for opportunities is that more homes are sold through this system than all others combined. It is the one system that most people are familiar with and therefore it may be least resisted by smaller or new investors.

The other reason I wanted to start with the MLS is because it is where I got much of my experience finding opportunities in the early days.

Direct to Seller

The place where I spend most of my energy identifying no money-down opportunities is "Direct to Seller". This is also where great deals can be found with the least resistance, and often the most flexibility. To get direct to the seller there are several low-cost and free ways of locating these opportunities.

Here are three approaches that we use today:

Sphere of Influence

If you want to be a successful investor you need to act like one starting today and that means letting everyone you know including friends, family, and associates know that you buy houses. When they hear about someone selling a property you would like to know before it goes on the market. The key is you want to get directly connected to the seller.

Networking

This is another great way of developing another sphere in an environment where people are already conditioned to provide your referrals. This can take some time for people in your networking groups to get to know and trust you, but once they do their referrals have a higher closing rate since you generally will be trusted by the seller due to the personal connection with the referring person. I like exclusive groups that only allow one person per industry in the group. However, I don't shy away from open groups as there are not many people who show up looking to buy homes. The key is you want to get directly connected to the seller.

Driving for Deals and Door-knocking

This is face-to-face prospecting. I have spent lots of time driving neighborhoods looking for potential opportunities. I look for a home that looks neglected, has maintenance issues, and may be the ugliest home in the neighborhood. Sometimes homeowners put big signs in the neighborhood saying come ask me – ok they say things like "estate sale," "moving sale," "for sale by owner" and even "garage sale."

I have stopped at homes that look like an opportunity knocking and so that's what I have done – go and knock on the door and ask if they want to sell.

Yes, I have purchased homes this way. I get a lot of noes but I also get yesses. The yesses make it worthwhile. When I first learned this technique from an investor friend, I thought no one would sell to someone who just knocked on their door. But you never know what circumstances have led to the property's disrepair or estate sale sign in the front yard.

Investor Groups

Another source is investor groups. Investor groups can be a good source for off-market properties. It may take some time to establish working relationships with some in these groups. If the goal is zero down then you will have to find the wholesalers that can help structure your purchases so that you can fully leverage the purchases.

Because this concept may be very new to many of these investors, this group can be more challenging than you would think. I find some investors that have been in the business for decades that don't like change or creativity.

As an investor, you may have access to some low-down-payment hard money options that may make the numbers work and these groups a profitable options as well.

CHAPTER 5

Creative Financing Case Studies

Case studies can be very informative and help us see what is possible. It shows what others have done and encourages us to know that we can do it too.

Case Study 1:

4 bed, 2 bath, 2200 square feet – Wrap

This transaction started nearly a year before it was acquired. The Seller was having financial difficulties but thought as many distressed sellers do, that they would get it corrected and so they rejected our cash offer. This is also a good example of never giving up because you hear the response “no”. Sometimes with distressed sellers the “no” really just means maybe.

When the seller finally asked us to help them keep from losing their house they were just weeks away from a default and foreclosure action.

This time around our offer looked much better and the seller was more flexible related to price and terms. What kind of terms? No Money Down!

Here is how we structured the deal to ensure our security:

We engaged an investor-friendly title company with an experienced investor transaction closing agent. We had the owner sign a warranty deed conveying their interest to us upon recordation. The seller signed our agreement wrapping the existing lien.

Here are three advantages of this type of creative financing which include:

1. **No money down or no down payment to the lender.** Since the terms of the purchase contract with the seller wrap or surround the existing lien, there is no down payment required.

   However, the seller may need or require some upfront payment to cover moving expenses, a down payment on a rental home, storage fees, some personal or family member loan. This is negotiable and the more motivated a seller is, the closer you get to a seller's need to move out.

2. **No qualification for the investor to take advantage of existing loan terms.** This generally means lower interest rates and no loan costs for the investor.

3. **Due-in-full date (balloon)** or if the wrap continues the full remaining term can be negotiated with the seller to give the investor time to complete a remodel, establish rental, sell with terms, etc...

The biggest risk I find with a wrap is the potential for the underlying lender to enforce a **due-on-sale** clause. If this was to occur the investor would be forced to refinance the property.

In this case study, we acquired it with no money down. Since it was a pending foreclosure and the seller had exhausted their financial resources the seller was without the resources to move out, store their personal belongings, or bring their existing mortgage current. We provided $2,375 for them to relocate and get a storage unit. We paid directly to the lender $2,711 to bring the lien current. This is probably a good place to note that we never give the money to the seller to bring the mortgage current. I have had associates do that and the money never got where it was supposed to go.

The last term we included was the carrot – we offered the seller a portion of our profit after all expenses, including the money we provided them to relocate.

We don't structure all our wrap offers the same. Each deal has its own unique set of facts and we adjust to provide a seller with what is fair and sufficently provides for their need. This is not a requirement but meets our company philosophy of building win-win transactions.

Case Study 2:

1 bed, 1 bath, 965 square feet – JV

This transaction started as a phone call for help to liquidate the contents of a downtown condo after the owner passed away. Sometimes people are asking for one thing when the solution to their problem is something else. I look to see how I can be that creative solution.

I suggested a couple of steps to the client. First, let's meet at the property so we can assess what they are requesting and second that we meet in person to discuss options. Due to the health of the local member of the estate, they were unable to do the walk-through in person and the other member did not live in the area. They agreed to allow me to go assess the condo and then stop by their house to meet afterward. Though I do remote transactions, if they are in the local area I always try to get a face-to-face meeting to build rapport with the seller. Rapport building can be achieved on the phone or by video meeting but face-to-face is still the best for me.

When we met I proposed a joint venture with the estate. I like joint ventures in that they limit my risk.

Unlike a wrap, the property's title remains in the name of the owner and we are secured by our joint venture agreement.

Again we engaged an investor-friendly title company with an experienced investor transaction closing agent who understood the terms of the joint-venture agreement.

For me, this meant no down payment and no leverage/lien payments.

Here are three advantages of this type of creative financing which include:

1. **No money down since the parties are in the deal together as partners.** The existing financing, if any would stay as it is. The only time in a joint venture that I offer any payment to the seller is if it advances, protects, or ensures the success of the project. This could include moving expenses, past-due utilities, homeowner association fees, etc… I try to avoid the seller from getting any personal benefit financially

up front and make them wait and be fully invested in the partnership portion of the agreement.

2. **No qualification for the investor to take advantage of existing loan terms since the seller remains on title.** If there is an existing lien, it would mean lower interest rates and no associated expenses to the investor.

3. **Seller remains responsible for insurance claims, utilities, etc...** Even if we negotiate to pay these expenses, we leave them in the owner's name and pay the companies directly.

The biggest risk I find with a joint venture is the potential risk that the owner decides they don't want to dispose of the property after all the work is complete. This could delay the disposition of the property while the agreement is enforced by the judicial process. I am glad that we have never had an owner force us to enforce the joint venture agreement.

In this case study, we got under contract with no money down. There was one underlying homeowner association lien that was pending foreclosure by the time the probate process had concluded and the estate contacted me. We negotiated with the law firm representing the association and paid the $13,036 to clear up the lien. It should be noted that many liens can wait until the sale closing to deal with but for others, you can receive negotiated discounts by addressing them upfront.

I also agreed to make the association payments going forward. This ensured I wouldn't have a hostile HOA to deal with in the future if the joint venture partner failed to make a payment, it also helped me negotiate the best payoff of the past due fees when I assured them I would be paying the fees on time going forward.

I also took on the responsibility for all the other expenses to ensure they were all maintained and paid on time moving forward.

The "carrot" in this transaction was to solve the problem that they originally contacted me about. What do you do with a condo full, and I mean full of personal property? Fortunately, the condo was relatively clean compared to the majority of homes we purchase but it had very little walking room. The previous owner was a collector of stuff. The items appeared to be nice, and likely quality and of value. Had I purchased this property outright, all the contents would have ended up in a dumpster or at some of my employees' homes. I always weigh how much time it will take to dumpster items versus sort-and-sell. Generally, the dumpster wins out! However, I have developed relationships with a couple of estate liquidation companies. I committed to the estate that I would bring in a company that would assess the value of the contents, catalog them, sell them, and provide them a check for the contents.

The trustee for the estate was ecstatic and so was I because it meant that when my crew showed up the condo would be empty and ready for deconstruction.

With joint venture opportunities, each one is structured a little differently. Like the wrap transactions, they all have their own unique set of facts. I work hard to provide a seller with a fair process and return. Not all investors look out for sellers's needs. It is my opinion that we as investors determine the returns we need, and consider the needs of others, we would have a better reputation as an industry, instead of being looked at as bottom feeders trying to take advantage of people. Back to our company philosophy of building win-win transactions.

CHAPTER 6

Risk Management & Legal Considerations

I cannot overstate the importance of managing risk in every one of your transactions. In a society that can sue anyone for anything, my theory is don't give anyone a reason, and if you give a reason, protect your downside. This is the reason why millions of Americans use Realtors® and attorneys to buy properties. These professionals have legal forms and understand deadlines and defaults.

Depending on the state you operate in will determine if you need a real estate lawyer to handle the closing of your transactions. At a minimum, you will need to develop a relationship with a good title company and agent who understands creative investing. If you are a remote investor that will operate in multiple states you may want to develop that relationship with a national or multistate company.

As an investor, you have the ability to ensure that others who prepare documents for you or documents you create yourself have some protective clauses. These clauses will be part of your risk management strategy. These examples are not exhaustive and this is why it is good to have relationships with legal and title professionals.

1. **Due diligence clause** – This clause allows you as the buyer/investor a period of time to inspect and verify the condition of a property. If you find issues beyond your expectation you can cancel the contract and receive a full refund of any earnest money you may have deposited.

2. **Earnest money clause** – In general, for a contract to be valid it will require consideration and as a gesture of good faith towards that consideration a

buyer would show their earnest intent by depositing earnest money with an escrow/title company.

As an investor, it is in your interest and as part of your risk management strategy that you deposit as little earnest money as you can get away with and still consummate the deal.

If you are involved in a traditional Realtor® involved transaction be prepared for a higher requested earnest money as that is part of what Realtors® are taught to do.

3. **Cancelation clause** – This clause is what I call the "get out of jail" clause. A properly written cancelation clause can allow you as an investor to terminate a transaction at any point in the transaction before closing.

   This clause is the just-in-case clause. Expect pushback if a Realtor® is involved but if you are working directly with the seller it is rare that the seller ever mentions it as a concern.

4. **Default clause** – What happens if you fail to fulfill some contingency and default and or are unable to fulfill the requirements of the negotiated contract? Your default clause if what minimizes the liability you have.

   If you do not have a properly worded default clause you could be sued for specific performance – forced to complete the transaction. However, if the default clause is properly written you may only be liable for liquid damages – the forfeiture of the earnest money as the only penalty for default.

   This in conjunction with the earnest money clause can mitigate your overall financial risk substantially.

CHAPTER 7

Zero Down Bonus

I decided to add this bonus chapter because of the overwhelming demand from people who said they thought by the title of the coaching program that I would teach them how to invest in real estate with absolutely no money out of pocket and no risk.

This hidden secret of top investors is the closest thing to no money out of pocket and zero risk.

Investors call this wealth-generating technique by several different names: Deal-digger, Birddog, or Referral Partner ("RP"). Whatever you call the opportunity it can be very profitable, low impact, and low monetary requirements. The main equity that is required is the ability to network and find opportunities.

The process works like this:

Step One: As an RP, you associate yourself with one or more investors looking to purchase homes for cash.

(See Chapter 4)

It is best to have the investor agreement in place before searching out your first deal because in most cases, time is a critical factor. Once you place the seed in a seller's mind that they can receive a cash offer and you take too long they may search out other cash offer investors via the internet and you will lose the deal searching for a partner investor.

Step Two: The next step is to determine what the investor you are going to be working with will pay you for your service. Each investor may have a different referral fee payment system. All compensation can be negotiated. Don't be surprised if a cash investor has a variable fee based on several factors.

Here are some examples:

Signed Contract Fee: General minimal amount for bringing the qualified lead.

Closed Contract Fee: This can vary based on acquisition cost and potential spread or ROI.

Disposition Fee: Some fix-and-flip and wholesale investors will pay either a split between closed and sold or provide a bonus when the property is disposed of.

Each cash investor knows what their average cost per acquisition costs them and generally, they will base the fees they pay an RP on this number.

Many of the cash investors I know pay anywhere between one thousand dollars and ten thousand dollars depending on the factors noted above. I just offered an RP twenty thousand to bring a particular deal together. The better the spread and terms the more generous the investor can be.

Step Three: The RP finds potential direct-to-seller investment opportunities.

You can use techniques found in listed in Chapter 4 to locate deals. I have several RPs, including Realtors® who are very good at finding these deals. I supply my RPs with my buying criteria and they hunt these kinds of deals. It is important if you are going to be an RP that you know the investor sweet spot for purchasing.

The investment for an RP in this type of no-money-down real estate investing is time, fuel, and maybe an iced tea or coffee.

Some RPs do spend minimal amounts on advertising by printing business cards, bandit signs, flyers, etc..

The last point that a PR should consider is using the referral fees they generate to begin active investing for themselves using the no-money-down process in this book and become another no-money-down real estate investor success story.

CHAPTER 9

Your Call to Action

On the journey of real estate investment, knowledge is indeed power, but ***action is the real catalyst for transformation***. As you close the final pages of this book, I urge you to embrace the profound truth that ***taking action is the bridge between where you are and where you want to be***. Every successful real estate investor started with a single step, a decision to move forward despite uncertainty or fear. Your success lies not just in the wisdom gleaned from these few pages, but in the actions you take to apply this knowledge in the real world.

Throughout history, great achievers have leaned on the guidance and wisdom of mentors to navigate the complexities of their business endeavors. **Mentorship accelerates your learning curve, provides invaluable insights, and empowers you with expert knowledge and experience to avoid costly mistakes.** It's the difference between stumbling blindly and deliberately moving towards your financial & personal goals with confidence. So, don't hesitate to seek out mentors who have walked the path you aspire to tread, and let their guidance illuminate your way forward.

I invite you to consider joining my one-on-one coaching program. When I first began in this industry, I could have saved myself from a lot of frustration and many lost deals by having a mentor who understands the process. In today's world, it has become an accepted best practice to seek out others who have a proven track record.

Our transformational coaching curriculum is designed to produce **maximum results in minimal time**. We support you in developing and refining the skills you need to succeed. We'll help you confront challenges head-on and develop a plan of action to overcome what has hindered you in the past.

<u>Our Coaching Clients Receive:</u>

- Personalized coaching curriculum designed specifically for your goals
- Weekly/ Monthly coaching sessions
- Specific action-oriented assignments
- Direct email access to your coach
- Confidential advice and accountability
- And much, much more!

Whether you're a novice investor seeking to take your first steps or a seasoned pro aiming to elevate your game, my coaching program and my new training course are designed to equip you with the tools, strategies, and mindset necessary to thrive in the world of real estate investment. The most successful investors aren't just the ones with the most knowledge, but those who dare to take action and seek guidance along the way.

Your journey towards financial freedom and abundance begins now. Don't let this moment pass you by. Reach out, take action, and let's embark on this transformative journey together.

Follow this link to schedule a
FREE vision session ($397 value)
with the author, Scott Whitwam:

www.NoMoneyDownOffer.com

Not sure if one-on-one coaching is for you? We get it. That's why we offer a FREE vision session with Coach Scott Whitwam. There's no obligation and it gives you an opportunity to ask questions and get a feel for what the process looks like. Remember, action is the real catalyst for transformation. Use the link above to take action and move one step closer to where you want to be... a successful real estate investor.

About the Author

Scott Whitwam is the founder of Whitwam Wealth. He has been a business owner for 40 years, in real estate for 35 years, and as a senior pastor for 24 years. Having closed 60 million in real estate, he has the expertise to show real estate investors the blueprint to financial abundance.

His innovative how-to systems have produced what he calls "Game-Changing Money" for his students. Scott believes in creating an environment of success using proven principles to affect both the **Mindset and Methods** for Wealth Building through Real Estate.

Scott brings a unique mix of skills to the coaching arena. His students benefit greatly from his entrepreneurial and real estate industry experience. He works with investors ranging from individuals to corporate organizations. Scott's experience and expertise add value at all levels of the student's journey. Scott has coached beginners and very sophisticated investors from frustration to success.

Scott has started fifteen successful businesses in a wide range of industries and currently owns six real estate-related businesses including the coaching company Whitwam Wealth Academy, where they formulate "Mindset and Methods, for Wealth Building through Real Estate." Since he is actively in business and investing in real estate, students benefit from his latest innovative, and little-known secrets.

Scott's students are coached in an environment of faith and encouraged to "treat your neighbor as yourself" – a win-win! Scott has been married to his wife Tina for 39 years, they have 3 children and 3 grandchildren.

Scott's other accomplishments include a Doctorate Degree, Author, Radio Host, Professor, and Event Speaker.

Here are the reasons you can depend on Scott Whitwam to help you live your full potential, start winning, gain confidence, be a success, fulfill your kingdom purpose, and build legacy:

- **REPUTABLE** – Scott Whitwam is a respected leader in his field and community.
- **EXPERIENCED** – His proudest accomplishment is the large number of long-term clients who put their trust in him year after year.
- **INTEGRITY** – Building a reputation of integrity takes years, but it takes only a second to lose. We don't believe in cutting corners. The foundation of our reputation is our commitment to do the right thing at all times, regardless of whether anyone is watching.
- **RESOURCES** – We offer a wide variety of **development and training** programs built on timeless principles that get results.
- **CUSTOMIZABLE** – All of our curriculum can be customized to specifically address your individual and organizational needs.

- **100% SATISFACTION GUARANTEE** – We want you to be completely satisfied with our services. We will do whatever it takes to make you happy. No hassles, no problems.

Follow this link to schedule a

FREE vision session ($397 value)

with the author, Scott Whitwam:

www.NoMoneyDownOffer.com

Author Disclaimer

Every effort has been made to accurately represent the skills, concepts, ideas, techniques, and "know-how" offered by Scott Whitwam and his potential. There is no guarantee that you will earn any money using the techniques and ideas in these materials. Examples in these materials are not to be interpreted as a promise or guarantee of earnings. Earning potential is entirely dependent on the person using our product, ideas and techniques. We do not purport this as a "get rich scheme."

Your level of success in attaining the results claimed in our materials depends on the time you devote to the program, ideas and techniques mentioned, your finances, knowledge and various skills. Since these factors differ according to individuals, we cannot guarantee your success or income level, nor are we responsible for any of your actions.

As always, we recommend you consult qualified financial and legal professionals before pursuing any actions to determine suitability for your specific situation.

Made in the USA
Middletown, DE
01 July 2024

56532613R00038